I LIKE WEIRD ANIMALS!

Bomb-Factory Beetles and Other Weird Insects

Series Science Consultant:
Dennis L. Claussen, PhD
Professor of Zoology
Miami University
Oxford, OH

Series Literacy Consultant:
Allan A. De Fina, PhD
Dean, College of Education
Professor of Literacy Education
New Jersey City University
Past President of the New Jersey Reading Association

Carmen Bredeson

CONTENTS

WORDS TO KNOW

abdomen (AB duh men)—The lower part of an insect's body.

dung—Another word for poop.

enemy (EH nuh mee)—An animal that tries to kill or is a threat to another animal.

nectar (NEK tur)—Sweet juice in flowers.

thorax (THOR aks)—The insect body part between the head and abdomen.

WEIRD INSECTS

There are insects everywhere on earth.

Butterflies, ants, and bees are a few types of insects.

All insects have six legs.

They also have three body parts: head, **thorax**, and **abdomen**.

Which weird insect is your favorite?

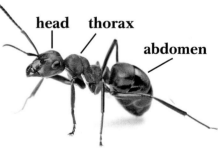

head   thorax

abdomen

This orchid mantis is an insect that looks like the orchid flower.

DUNG BEETLE

Dung beetles eat nothing but POOP!

Some dig right into a fresh pile.

Others roll the poop into balls.

They bury poop balls in the ground to eat later.

Dung beetles even try to steal poop balls from each other.

GIANT WETA

Giant wetas are a kind of grasshopper, but they are too big to fly or jump.

They can grow to be six inches long!

Giant wetas are gentle insects.

You can hold one in your hand and it will not bite.

BOMBARDIER BEETLE

If an **enemy** gets too close to the bombardier (bahm buh DEER) beetle, it had better watch out!

The beetle has a bomb factory in its body.

It mixes two juices together that get VERY hot.

Then the beetle sprays its enemy.

The hot juice can kill the enemy.

ARMY ANT

Thousands of army ants march in long, long lines.

What happens when the ants come to water?

Some of the ants hook their legs together.

They build a living bridge.

The other ants crawl across the bridge.

MOTHER OF PEARL CATERPILLAR

UH-OH! Here comes trouble.

To escape danger, the caterpillar hooks its rear end to the ground.

Then it flips back and makes a circle with its body.

ZOOM! The caterpillar rolls away like a green wheel.

HONEYPOT ANT

Worker ants bring **nectar** for the other honeypot ants to eat.

First the ants store the nectar in their bodies.

Their abdomens swell to the size of grapes.

Then they spit up the nectar for the other ants to eat.

This ant's abdomen is full of nectar.

Can you spot the giant walking sticks?

GIANT WALKING STICK

A walking stick looks just like a branch with legs.

It hides in the trees and bushes.

Giant walking sticks can grow to be more than twenty inches long!

That is as long as a t-ball bat.

POND SKATER

Pond skaters can run on TOP of the water.

They do not sink.

The pond skater's long middle legs paddle across the water.

The back legs steer left and right.

Short front legs catch little insects for the pond skater to eat.

LEARN MORE

Books

Arlon, Penelope. *Insect*. New York: DK Publishing, 2006.

Taylor, Barbara. *Insects*. Boston: Kingfisher, 2008.

Twist, Clint. *Dung Beetles*. Strongville, Ohio: Gareth Stevens Publishing, 2005.

LEARN MORE

Web Sites

Enchanted Learning
www.enchantedlearning.com/themes/insects.shtml

Let's Talk About Insects
www.urbanext.uiuc.edu/insects/

INDEX

For my weird siblings: Ralph, Jack, and Renee

Enslow Elementary, an imprint of Enslow Publishers, Inc.
Enslow Elementary® is a registered trademark of Enslow Publishers, Inc.

Library of Congress Cataloging-in-Publication Data

Bredeson, Carmen.
  Bomb-factory beetles and other weird insects / Carmen Bredeson.
    p. cm.—(I like weird animals!)
  Summary: "Provides young readers with facts about several strange insects"—Provided by publisher.
  ISBN-13: 978-0-7660-3123-4
  ISBN-10: 0-7660-3123-3
  1. Insects—Miscellanea—Juvenile literature. I. Title.
  QL467.2.B734 2009
  595.7—dc22

                    2008021497

Printed in the United States of America

10 9 8 7 6 5 4 3 2 1

♻ Enslow Publishers, Inc., is committed to printing our books on recycled paper. The paper in every book contains 10% to 30% post-consumer waste (PCW). The cover board on the outside of each book contains 100% PCW. Our goal is to do our part to help young people and the environment too!

Photo Credits: © Alex Wild Photography, p. 13; ANT Photo Library/Photo Researchers, Inc., p. 17; © Dr. John Brackenbury/Photo Researchers, Inc., p. 15; © Dr. Thomas Eisner/Visuals Unlimited, pp. 1, 10; © Emil Enchev/Alamy, pp. 2, 6; © Ingo Arndt/Minden Pictures, p. 21; © Ingrid Vissesr/Hedgehog House/Minden Pictures, p. 9; © National Geographic/Getty Images, p. 18; © Rod Clarke/John Downer Produ/naturepl.com, p. 14; Shutterstock, p. 4; © Thomas Marent/Minden Pictures, p. 5; © Tim Edwards/naturepl.com, p. 8.

Cover Photo: © Dr. Thomas Eisner/Visuals Unlimited

Note to Parents and Teachers: The *I Like Weird Animals!* series supports the National Science Education Standards for K–4 science. The Words to Know section introduces subject-specific vocabulary words, including pronunciation and definitions. Early readers may need help with these new words.

Enslow Elementary
an imprint of
E **Enslow Publishers, Inc.**
40 Industrial Road
Box 398
Berkeley Heights, NJ 07922
USA
http://www.enslow.com